DINOSAURS

This Edition first published 2002 by
MENTOR BOOKS
43 Furze Road • Sandyford Industrial Estate • Dublin 18.
Tel. (01) 295 2112/3 • Fax. (01) 295 2114
e-mail: admin@mentorbooks.ie • www.mentorbooks.ie

ISBN: 1-84210-145-5

Design and layout by Kathryn McKinney
Printed in Ireland by ColourBooks

T-REX

Draw a circle and basic head shape.

Draw in eyes, mouth and snout.

Add final detail.

* T-Rex is one tough customer!

PARASAUROLOPHUS

Draw a pear shape
and indicate the
horn and snout.

Always put in
guide lines
with a pencil.

Add final detail.

PTERANODON

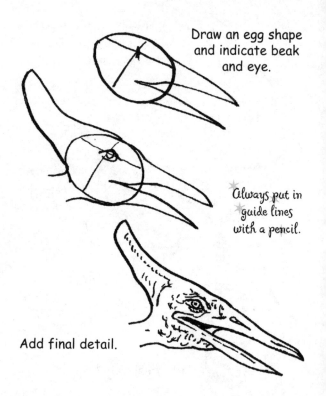

Draw an egg shape
and indicate beak
and eye.

*Always put in
guide lines
with a pencil.

Add final detail.

IGUANODON

Draw a square and basic head shape.

Draw in eyes, mouth and snout.

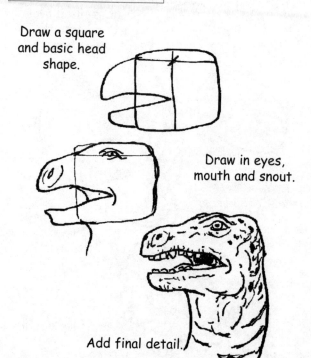

Add final detail.

TRICERATOPS

Draw a tilted oval and indicate the bony plate.

Draw in eyes, snout and horns.

Add final detail.

MAIASAURA

Draw a circle and indicate eyes, snout and neck.

Always put in guide lines with a pencil.

Add final detail.

Did you know that Maiasaura means 'Good Mother Lizard'?

For rough sketches use soft pencils such as H,B or 2B.

1. Draw egg shapes. Indicate the neck, legs and tail.

HOW TO DRAW A STEGOSAURUS

2. Work up the body shape as shown.

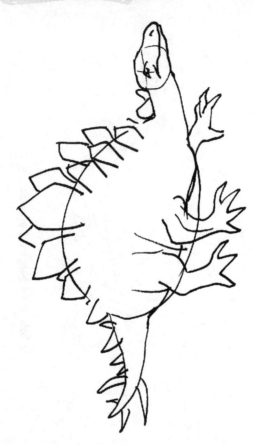

3. Now add bony plates on the back and tail, and detail to the face.

HOW TO DRAW A STEGOSAURUS

4. Finish with a felt-tip marker. Rub out all your pencil lines.

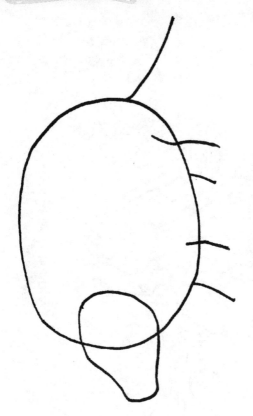

1. Draw rough shapes for the body and head. Indicate the legs and tail.

HOW TO DRAW A TRICERATOPS

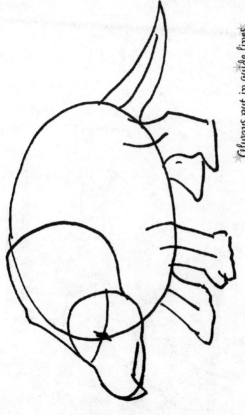

Always put in guide lines with a pencil.

2. Work up the body shape as shown.

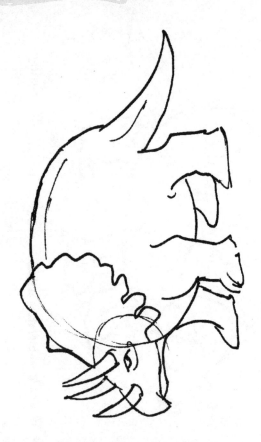

3. Add horns and more detail to the bony plate and body.

HOW TO DRAW A TRICERATOPS

4. Finish with a felt-tip marker.
Rub out all your pencil lines.

1. Begin with egg shapes. Indicate the arms, legs and tail.

Always put in guide lines
with a pencil.

2. Work up the body shape as shown.

This is a good stage to make changes or alterations.

3. Try to get character and movement into the drawing.

HOW TO DRAW A T-REX

T-Rex is on the
✳rampage!✳

**3. Finish with a felt-tip marker.
Rub out all your pencil lines.**

1. Draw rough shapes for the body and head. Indicate the legs and beak.

HOW TO DRAW A PTEROSAUR

Always put in guide lines with a pencil.

2. Work up the body shape as shown.

3. Add more detail.

HOW TO DRAW A PTEROSAUR

Pterosaurs were not dinosaurs,
but flying lizards.
(But they're still fun to draw!)

**4. Finish with a felt-tip marker.
Rub out all your pencil lines.**

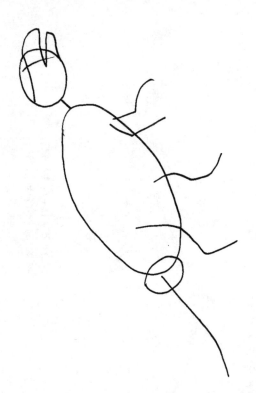

1. Draw circle and egg shapes for the body. Indicate the legs and tail.

HOW TO DRAW AN ALLOSAURUS

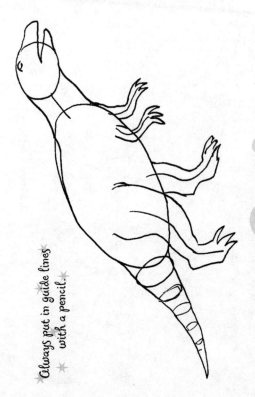

Always put in guide lines with a pencil.

2. Work up the body shape as shown.

This is a good stage to make changes or alterations.

3. Add more detail.

HOW TO DRAW AN ALLOSAURUS

4. Finish with a felt-tip marker. Rub out all your pencil lines.

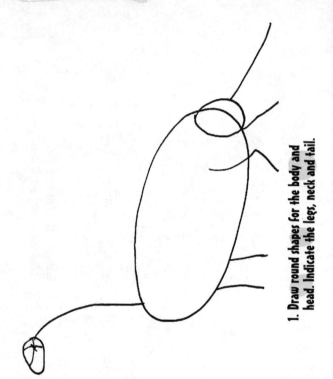

1. Draw round shapes for the body and head. Indicate the legs, neck and tail.

HOW TO DRAW A DIPLODOCUS

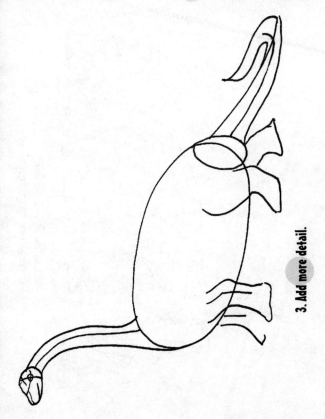

3. Add more detail.

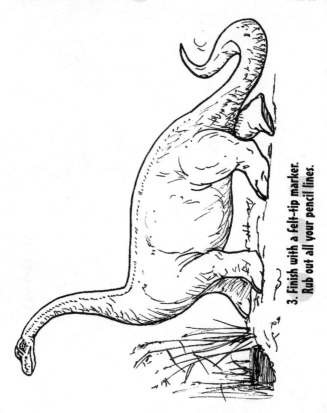

3. Finish with a felt-tip marker. Rub out all your pencil lines.

HOW TO DRAW A DEINONYCHUS

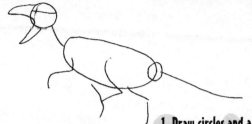

1. Draw circles and a sausage shape. Indicate the legs and neck.

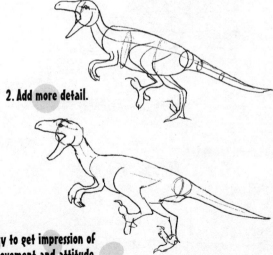

2. Add more detail.

3. Try to get impression of movement and attitude.

HAVE FUN !